BOA
EDITIONS LTD

Tracing the Horse

Tracing the Horse

poems by

Diana Marie Delgado

A. Poulin, Jr. New Poets of America Series, No. 43

BOA Editions, Ltd. ℰ Rochester, NY ℰ 2019

First Edition
19 20 21 22 7 6 5 4 3 2 1

For information about permission to reuse any material from this book, please
contact The Permissions Company at www.permissionscompany.com or e-mail
permdude@gmail.com.

Publications by BOA Editions, Ltd.—a not-for-profit corporation
under section 501 (c) (3) of the United States Internal Revenue Code—
are made possible with funds from a variety of sources, including
public funds from the Literature Program of the National Endowment
for the Arts; the New York State Council on the Arts, a state agency;
and the County of Monroe, NY. Private funding sources include the
Max and Marian Farash Charitable Foundation; the Mary S. Mulligan
Charitable Trust; the Rochester Area Community Foundation;
the Ames-Amzalak Memorial Trust in memory of Henry Ames,
Semon Amzalak, and Dan Amzalak; the LGBT Fund of Greater Rochester; and
contributions from many individuals nationwide. See Colophon on page 72 for
special individual acknowledgments.

NATIONAL
ENDOWMENT
for the ARTS
arts.gov

State of the Arts

NYSCA

Cover Design: Daphne Morrissey
Cover Photograph: Courtesy of Diana Marie Delgado
Interior Design and Composition: Richard Foerster
BOA Logo: Mirko

Library of Congress Cataloging-in-Publication Data

Names: Delgado, Diana Marie, 1975– author.
Title: Tracing the horse / poems by Diana Marie Delgado.
Description: First edition. | Rochester, NY : BOA Editions, Ltd., 2019. |
  Series: New poets of America series ; no. 43
Identifiers: LCCN 2019019270| ISBN 9781942683872 (pbk.) | ISBN
9781942683889 (ebk.)
Classification: LCC PS3604.E44386 A6 2019 | DDC 811/.6—dc23 LC record
available at https://lccn.loc.gov/2019019270

BOA Editions, Ltd.
250 North Goodman Street, Suite 306
Rochester, NY 14607
www.boaeditions.org
A. Poulin, Jr., Founder (1938–1996)

Contents

§

§

Foreword

La Puente in the San Gabriel Valley of Los Angeles County is a barrio like any other—and also unlike any other. Diana Marie Delgado has discovered the poetry in its fissures, the upturned sidewalks, the stucco-over-wood-frame homes, the grassless lawns, and heroin-fed angst that breathes beneath its disarming squat apartments and two-room houses and garages crammed with family.

> After robbing H&H Liquor, drowsy with blood, they hide in the
> cellar, and dream the same thing: gang fame.
>
> Driving to the methadone clinic: You know too much about us.
> Addicts are lucky: they get to focus on one thing their entire life.

In 60 years the SGV went from orange and walnut groves, with 100 migrant communities, mostly Mexican, with no sidewalks, unpaved roads, and shacks, to white suburbs with shopping malls, drive-ins, and parks, dotted with factories and warehouses, to a cultural hodgepodge of townhouses, McMansions, and kanji-lettered storefronts. Due to this new kind of gentrification, white flight and other factors, the SGV now has more Asians—from Japan, Taiwan, Hong Kong, Korea, and mainland China—than any other area of the United States. The largest Buddhist and Hindu temples in the country have a home here. Today it's also 70 percent Mexican and Central American.

The new America—unsaved by a jagged prosperity, a roller-coaster economy, and increasingly detached politics. Let's try poetry.

Reading Diana Marie Delgado, I feel the bones she rattles, the blood currents she rides, the imagery and language that spiral up the crushed and diminished voices. Witness this excerpt:

> When no one could
> decipher the speaker,
>
> I spoke,

Mom, come sit at the table
with me, pat down my hair.

In the bedroom,
where all things

are said with a sigh,
I do have more fun,

I can't move—

Or this:

The plumes of the avocado are sick.

Dad cuts roses with a hatchet.

In hell, there's nothing but crocodiles

and fathers. In Mexico, the Devil is handsome

and smiles in all his photographs. He has one wife,

two daughters, three sons, but no mother.

He rakes leaves then fixes umbrellas,

occasionally throws back his head and sings.

DMD of the SGV. Yes, she's lived in other cities—New York City and Tucson among others. But here she chants in mythic mode the inexpressible in ways that hold us far beyond a reading, or black ink on a bleached page, or a syllable enraptured with suicide and the pull of living through that silent scream.

Enough of what haunts me. Read Diana Marie Delgado.

—Luis J. Rodriguez
San Fernando, CA

Tracing the Horse

Little Swan

Most nights I'm face to face with the stars.
No one is more afraid of this than me.

So I find places to lie down
and signify. I'm practicing a play

where my brother's doing time in prison
and I'm locked out of the house.

Talking is like falling down or
watching your uncle

pull himself into his wheelchair,
the sun moving over

his arms like a blessing.
At least I had a mother

who could sew her name
into my hair.

I want to lie in her stomach again,
understand the drive

to hurt something young,
wild with sky.

My father and brother enter,
and one of them says,

You should start this story
with the death of a child.

They Chopped Down the Tree I Used to Lie Under and Count Stars With

I tape a red telephone to its ear so the fetus appears to speak to someone.

Write about a time when you were forced and didn't want to.

The man from the dairy, dick in both hands, like it's champagne.

Wearing paper-blue slippers, I follow a nurse into a room lined with cots.

The doctor: Want to know what it is?

Look into the picture, see yourself before any of this happened.

I dream, I tell Marcos, of combat; I reach down and weapons appear.

A car window rolls down. *¿Hablas español?*

One day you'll think of men—and it will be like looking at a gray wall.

Doesn't "embarrassed" sound like "embarazada" in Spanish?

The phone rings, it's the Devil—I forgot to tie up the dog.

Overheard in Mexico: What's a girl with seven brothers?

On *General Hospital*, Luke raped Laura, and then they fell in love.

Inside the Impala's trunk: clubs and maces.

I'm kissing a boy in his car, below a streetlamp vibrating with moths.

I pretend to lie in sand, be part ocean, dust from a candy cigarette.

Spanish feels like eating roses sprinkled with lime;

English, peeling potatoes, barefoot.

A wedding party, and Dad, passing, honks. Suckers!

Grandpa, putting money in my hands: Ride that bike like the wind.

When you see yourself is there an observer?

A boyfriend: You blacked out. We had sex to calm you down.

Your pussy's like a clamshell, it closes like a purse.

I rode through stars, through streets where the wind talked to us.

Savage birds called out; I looked up and listened.

House Where Wisteria Grew

When no one could
decipher the speaker,

I spoke,

Mom, come sit at the table
with me, pat down my hair.

In the bedroom,
where all things

are said with a sigh,
I do have more fun,

I can't move—

The day I asked
We ready to leave:

Go you're old enough.

She was many people then
all of them in love.

Free Cheese and Butter

Mom's good at waiting.
We can stand for hours

but she won't tie and untie
shoelaces like my brother

who yanks pigtails and pinches
with monkey hands,

that smell of sweaty nickels.
I practice her signature in the air,

a clump of curlicues,
all the round letters of the alphabet.

My brother tugs my arm,
points to the end of the line.

Patty Garcia's there with
teeth like the keys

on Mr. Sergio's piano, eyes
so big she blinks a lot

to keep them in. At school,
she's who we chase.

Twelve Trees

The plumes of the avocado are sick.

Dad cuts roses with a hatchet.

In hell, there's nothing but crocodiles

and fathers. In Mexico, the Devil is handsome

and smiles in all his photographs. He has one wife,

two daughters, three sons, but no mother.

He rakes leaves then fixes umbrellas,

occasionally throws back his head and sings.

Before the Moon Tangles Your Hair

Mom follows me around the room like a cat, sits next to me, expecting my father, expecting change. After she kicks him out, he works out at La Puente Gym with Samoans who shave his head and turn him into one of them: young, tall, fierce. Everyone waits for something to hallow, but his wait is longest. My mother has a dream where the Devil, disguised as smoke, comes down from the attic, and twisting around and around her, leaves her unable to cry out.

The Sea Is Farther Than Thought

In church, the boys have so much
light, plants grow towards them.
My aunt handed me an organdy
fan and said: Hold this if you're frightened
or want to lose yourself—the Devil
can dance like a goddamn dream.

There are three things on Earth
to point to: the sun, the moon, and
the television. I can locate one of these.
My brother walked into a garage
with a needle taped to a battery
and emerged with his stomach

tattooed. I don't think I'll touch a face
like that again. Across the street, wetbacks
sleep five to a room and sweep
and water their dirt, while children send
canoes without oars down the Hudson.
Let me explain Westward Expansion:

Snow unfolded over a wagon train
of nine and nothing without wings survived.
The sea is farther than thought. He answered
the door holding a rag to his neck
and we kissed on the service porch
near a pit bull that'd just won a fight.

Sometimes my father whittles
for my mother in front of a bonfire, the vein
searching his thigh, Corinthian-blue.
To be honest, I called because there was snow

in my glove, not because I missed you.
If the original tunnel of the body

is the mouth, I've never had one.
As a girl I kept suede horses
and a hairbrush inside a blond toy-box.
One day my face will refuse to turn away.
Some people like poison.
I kneeled every time I opened it.

Wolf (1)

Had a lighter in his room, a heater that buzzed
like an electric heart; powdered doughnuts,

stool softeners, water pills, rubbing alcohol, Q-tips, cotton
balls, plastic gloves, baby powder;

Polaroids of women standing behind him while he sat,
hands folded in his lap,

a Mexican blanket draped over his wheelchair. He had old
newspapers, diabetic socks, a Dodger cap

and a jar of change someone stole after his wake
when they came to clean his room.

House of Stars

Maria's standing like a man,
one hundred pounds

poured into a slippery T-shirt
the color of mushrooms,

helping Joey tune the
'67 Pontiac

he'll sell for two thousand
the year he's out of work.

They build pyramids
in our home, teach

why the Aztecs
held so many hearts.

In the bathroom,
a motor roars,

Dad's body
constantly oiled.

Tracing the Horse

I'm riding a horse I can't stop drawing,
a wild one with a whip for a tail.

It's a song in a dream
whose words burn
my hands like light.

　　　...

The moon's gone down again.

If you play cards at night,
the Devil pulls up a chair, plays with you.

I believe my Mother—I'm ten.

　　　...

She told me study the moon.

Take a picture and tell the world
what it means, only I wasn't sure

what the moon would say,
especially to me; I couldn't

look out the window.

　　　...

We drove to Ensenada,
sailed to an island of squid

that, once hooked,
stained the Pacific.

Over that ocean a dark
so dark it was blue.

     ...

Maybe Mom's the horse
because aren't horses beautiful,
can't they kill a man if spooked?

     ...

Mr. Wyrick reads from
the Bible, ties Joseph
to his desk like the pigs
I've seen slaughtered
for holy communion.

     ...

The Devil grabs my feet
to cover them in pollen.

I should stop talking to him.

He turned me into a crow,
put music in me, told me why our plum tree
was called *Purple Heart*.

     ...

Mom brushes my hair
asks me to tell time;

when I get it wrong,
she slaps me.

    …

On the ocean, gulls made space
for sunlight as we followed him

into the garage to gut
barracuda, shoo flies.

    …

I take a book home, read and return it;
a star is put next to my name.

I never read the whole book, just parts,
words in a row, I read for feelings.

§

Late-Night Talks with Men I Think I Trust

He's made me smaller, taken
fingernails and spoken
words that force me to wake

where plum trees don't give
and dogs, tied to houses with rope,
are shot through with silver.

His sisters battered our door
with a hatchet and telescope
found at a yard sale.

"In a home, too much green
makes one lose facility."

"If you hear owls laughing outside your house,
someone's bewitched you,"

Grandmother warned me, grabbed
cats by their tails, threw them
over fences.

At night, we folded tortillas
into our mouths, pulled splinters
from our palms.

No one spoke above the TV
unless we spilled or wanted more.

Through cattails, children led horses.
Dogs gnawed on shards of bone.

We belong to these conversations.

That's why it's taken me this long to write his name.

I did what no one's ever done:
I met my father.

Desire Is a Road

Spend enough time on your knees
and you become sacred.

My father, who palmed corsets, was like this.

He'd shoot up, present something brilliant in his voice
then scratch his face, proclaim: Not here.

My mother, more taken with plans than
results, thought him a find, hot like dice,
hair-trigger too.

Whenever I asked her for advice
she'd shrug, point to the elms:

I used to live over there,
steal peaches for Carmen.

This is how my mother taught me
the difference between desire and the sea,

one is always bigger.

Primos

After the wedding reception, near the dumpsters where the man who ran the parties told us to throw the trash, I see two older cousins kissing; when my headlights catch their faces, they turn, their eyes aglow.

Natural History

We sit at the edge of my bed, pull off my clothes.
The dollar is strong and scientists create an igloo

for a man who's been dead over 10,000 years.
His last meal: acorns and venison. Summer was sweet—

you had gone. I practiced sleeping, first watched
Rodney King's beating on videotape, then the fossil

of a Mesozoic bird, curled inside its egg like an eyelash,
declared the most ancient unborn.

Bridge Called Water

I wrote hard
on paper

at the bottom
of a pool

near a canyon
where the stars

slid onto their bellies
like fish.

I wrote:

    ...

I went through
the mountain

through the leaves
of La Puente

to see the moon
but too late

too long ago
to walk on glass.

    ...

Near those years
when the house fell on me

my father told me
draw Mom

in bed with
another man.

    …

From a plum tree

the sounds of branches
fall like fruit

I'm older
no longer afraid

my voice, water
from a well

where someone was always
running into my room

asking, what's wrong?

In the Romantic Longhand of the Night

Let's kneel on gravel, tear apart the lace

of fruit, blade the wool from lambs

who kiss hard, eat the meadow's changing face.

Late, the lark's a con of hands that frown

aloud and spin tales free of green.

Let's break into picnics over the phone, befriending men

who crack safes and win ribbons for pigs that curry in the grain.

Let's soap each face locked in a bathroom,

slip them a letter written in the night's romantic longhand.

Let's fake it the right way, draped in the right light

for the wrong person. Although we say we aren't,

we're seeking the tricky algorithm

of travel, boys who wager swans first

and survive on cobwebs and capture.

Prayer for What's in Me to Finally Come Out

I want to smoke weed on Easter,

walk with cousins up P. Hill

and, passing 7-Eleven, look into

the sweet and smoky houses of the middle class

and think you never know. I want to fade

in the doorway of the house I grew up in,

understand why the light in my dad's body

after the needle's tucked in is orange

on a river so silver I can barely see him.

I want to wear a yellow sundress

in the hallway of a rented house,

holding what I meant to send you

that summer I bought my first car

and Y.A. shaved my brother's head,

replacing his name with a number.

I want to walk P. Hill before

my brother was shot and the neighbors

carried him in on a dining room chair

to lay him on my mother's bed,

where later, waking, he yelled,

"Mom! Bring me my pills!"

The Kind of Light I Give Off Isn't Going to Last

There should be somewhere to put the heart when it dies. If only I can hear you opening again, a flower. But nothing is ever real. Everything dies. The heart of a woman shuts so tight when pierced it waters. I was jealous. His girlfriend had horses (and what girl doesn't want to come home and ride horses?). The wind said you'd fly back but men grow damaged from cutting vines that blossom in the dark. I know what you want: a burial inside me. Have you ever opened an apricot, warmed by the sun, and found worms?

Maria

Let's admit there was never going to be a baby, let
alone the one we talked about that year. She would
have been beautiful, with long feet, a bad temper.

Lucky You

There will be an epic full of
the honest weather we made.

It will discuss in detail
the moon, how it set inside me,
and how carefully
I give you this light.

All absence is large,
a stretch of spine you can
never touch.

Horses on the Radio

Lacan is on the air; his subject, the body.
He fattens the sensational value of tattoos.

He's vague about the nature of sex and how to undo the phallus.
Says there is sex even when things enter bad and with scorch.

He recommends a husband, yet is unclear
on whether the goal is glass or wine.

He understands that language makes phone calls no one answers.

Some Guy I Liked Who Dated Strippers

You have sleep in your eyes as we climb the hill to the Sheraton Hotel in your mini truck. The golf course glistens on both sides, and we sit beneath an oak tree. When you grab my hand every hormone bothers me: you're not my tomorrow. It's 3 a.m. The sprinklers turn on, and your jacket is covered with watery diamonds.

Where I Drown

There are games to play
as a skeleton.

Fall asleep and become
a marigold for the dead,

mummy folded so tightly,
ants befriend you.

But my favorite
part that's taught,

is that Dad
never stops.

Notes for White Girls

Roaches bubbling out of drawers and cabinets, so many that each time a boyfriend asked for something to eat, I'd head to the kitchen, turn on the light, and squash with my hand whatever I saw running. They thought I had them sit in the living room because I liked serving them. Life as a girl in a Mexican family can feel different. Sometimes like you're not part of the family.

Songs of Escape

1

Our house: two doors,
a window that never opens.

2

A nurse shines a penlight
in each eye, nods when I answer.

My hair is falling out again.
The doctor doesn't know why.

God does; so does Mom.

3

I lean over a sink
the color of seashells,
cutting myself,

proving I can sweat
into the symptom,

watch the doves
pour out of me.

4

Dad traps the calico tabby that killed our bird,
pushes her into a plastic bag,
then into the gutter,
so she'll learn.

5

I sit at the kitchen table
misspelling pleas for help:

Peeple to Run From

Joey Bulldog
Juice
Tonito
Wolf
Silent
Bugsy
Bewilder
El Scorpion

6

Come winter, I sing.

I carry a red flame
in my nightgown pocket,
am slapped until I learn
to ask for softer fruit
 semen, egg yolk, blood.

Ordinary things that girls
are forced to swallow.

7

Men are the only islands
I've ever lived on.
I'll never get away.

8

I turn in sleep,
but parts of me won't.

They stay very still—
someone is always touching me.

9

Easter, the sky a full-blown rose.

From under the shade
of a loquat tree,

my uncle Wolf says:

You're writing a ghost story.
A book for a man who's never gonna come.

Dream Obituary

Last night, my mother came to me,
holding my youngest brother.

The ends of her body had disappeared.

Now in the middle of my life
my journey is to forgive
everything that's happened.

§

Who Makes Love to Us After We Die

I turn on the radio and hear voices, girls becoming women after tragedy. Talk about dreams! His heart was covered in a thin shell the color of moon and when touched, I grew old. The best movies have a philosophy (Dorothy, after being subjected to girl-on-girl violence, is rescued). Someone hanged himself on that set, a man who loved but couldn't have a certain woman. Management claimed it was a bird. The best movies begin with an encounter and end with someone setting someone free. In Coppola's *Dracula* the camera chases women across a garden until they kiss. The man I loved, after many years, asked me to choke him in bed; later, cleaning a kitchen cabinet, I found a recipe he'd carved into the wood, and I had a hard time believing him.

Juice

driving to Santa Anita Race Track, talking black-and-white photography:
In high school, I took a picture of a Dalmatian next to a fire hydrant.

It won first place—I set it up and everything. The day he OD'd
I didn't remember that he wore military fatigues, lived with his mom

and had long slender fingers that curled around the steering wheel
like sunlight in June. I remember him telling me:

I was young, photographing the world.

El Scorpion

Grandpa woke just as the doctor came in, "Mrs. Lopez, we'll have to move your husband to hospice," and Grandma, who never learned English, asked, "*¿Que dijo, Felipe?*" and Grandpa answered, "Stupid, that means I'm going to die!"

Firebird

Chain steering wheel, screwdriver in the glove box we used to pick the alternator 'til it sparked when it died and dad would pop the hood, point the flashlight, and yell to mom—*pump the fuckin gas*—until the engine would roar, and we'd be gone.

Wolf (2)

Wolf can't walk
so he sends me to the liquor store for
Sisco and a cigarette.

"Babe, make sure it's the green one,
orange gives a bad buzz."

I look up and the sun is flashing
pavement grains aglitter.

He lifts the cushion of his wheelchair,
shows me a gun wrapped in shoeshine rags.

"Just in case," he says, pointing
its barrel toward a cawing field

across the street. Weeks had passed
since the fire. Still, crows circled.

Correspondence

Brother, deep in the moth hour, still no altar to speak of:
Everyone's got a life they can't stop; time passes, nothing survives.

The real me slipped out like a hiccup, and he marooned himself
in the arms of another girl's couch. *I have a book for you*

about life and a real-time G doing it. Mom's fine, breaking crooked
as an eggshell; Dad the same teething crocodile.

I've never seen so much sad architecture. Remember when the yard froze
white and Mom tied plastic over our shoes?

This is the only place that's ever felt like home. I hope you get this letter
before lights out . . . or have you learned to read in the dark?

Man of the House

My brother brings home diamonds

Mom scratches against
the coffee table glass.

I'm on the couch, reading *The Stand*

when he walks in after stealing
a woman's purse.

Later, I watch him wrap
a shotgun in a blanket,

place it in the trunk
of Danny's car.

Dad, from the bedroom:

Who does he think he is
bringing home finery?

Greenbriar Lane

How long are we going to have this problem with rent?
Someone asks. I'm on the back patio planting begonias
in coffee-black earth. My job is to bring beautiful
things back to life. When I hear, through the windows,
men call my name, I turn—they're not there.

Amiga

We were in front of Kmart when I called your boyfriend an asshole for beating you up and you told me if I said anything bad about him again, you'd never speak to me.

In the Starlight of an Arrest

I communicated by dividing my face into dozens of complicated shapes. In one room, projected on the walls, were films my brother had made. When I asked what was wrong, Mom showed me a Polaroid he'd taken in prison: They poisoned him. "Dad!" I called into the hallway where he appeared covered in blankets, a ghost, "You said you were going to protect him."

Vecino Drive

Once Mom got the nerve to scream, "Stop hitting her" from the top of the steps, only for Dad to get out of bed, yank her in: It's none of your business.

The Playboy Lounge

They find him dead,
one hand poking

through the trash,
fingers unfurled

like dahlias
when they try

to cup the light.

Never Mind I'm Dead

Come back with me
to the ruins.
We will look
through family
photographs;
I can show you
what the wind
and I did.
Who keeps
the stars
from falling
out of the sky?
Macho, our dog,
used to curl up
on the patio
and yawn.
I remember
playing on the grass
when Mom came to spank me
and he jumped up—
bit her hand.

La Puente

Letter from Corcoran Prison: Please deposit $1,500 into the P.O. Box
of Debra C.—the Mafia's going to kill me.

After 911 they asked the Chicanos in prison and one of them raised
his hand: How do you think we took it? We're Americans.

Mule Creek, Delano, Chowchilla, Avenal, Pelican Bay, Calipatria,
Centinela, Ironwood, Solano, Wasco, Corcoran, Tehachapi.

California has a lot of prisons, all with beautiful names.

A cop I'm dating charges a gang member with possession: I
understand you—the people I arrest remind me of your family.

Dad's arm out the car window: You're going to have a hard time
finding a man.

On my brother's 40th birthday: I played gin rummy with Birdman.
Manson's worth money, the court signs his name with a stamp.

After robbing H&H Liquor, drowsy with blood, they hide in the
cellar, and dream the same thing: gang fame.

Driving to the methadone clinic: You know too much about us.
Addicts are lucky: they get to focus on one thing their entire life.

Dad's drunk: Cornell, Princeton, Pepperdine? The names sound like
exotic spices! Where you going to?

On a bench at La Puente Park: Call my manager—he stashed ten thousand
for me. From his backpack he pulls a dead watch.

I lived next to a train crossing on Valley Blvd, the sky above pink-
   and-gold stars.

Summers were horses traced on denim; my youth unfolding,
   paper fan.

Acknowledgments

I would like to thankfully acknowledge the following publications for publishing the below poems, some in earlier form:

Academy of American Poets: "Bridge Called Water" and "Who Makes Love to Us After We Die";
BorderSenses: "Wolf (2)";
Fourteen Hills: "Songs of Escape";
Great River Review: "Before the Moon Tangles Your Hair";
Ilanot Review: "Wolf (1)";
Indiana Review: "The Sea Is Farther Than Thought";
Laurel Review: "Correspondence";
Lumina: "Twelve Trees";
The Pebble Lake Review: "Little Swan";
Perihelion: "Desire Is a Road";
Pilgrimage: "Amiga" and "Some Guy I Liked Who Dated Strippers";
Ploughshares: "Late-Night Talks with Men I Think I Trust";
Prairie Schooner: "House Where Wisteria Grew";
Rhetoric and Chicana/o Studies Reader: "The Playboy Lounge";
Slice: "In the Starlight of an Arrest";
Smartish Pace: "Free Cheese and Butter";
Tin House: "They Chopped Down the Tree I Used to Lie Under and Count Stars With";
TriQuarterly: "Notes for White Girls" and "Maria";
West Branch: "Tracing the Horse" and "La Puente."

Too many people to name, give thanks to, who cared for and supported the development, writing, re-writing, and completion of this book. In particular, gracias to Lorna Dee Cervantes, who ferried me to Isla Mujeres and told me I have a bird inside, "let it sing"; Rigoberto González for tough talks but believing too; Luis J. Rodriguez, who inspired me to honor my first agreement—to writing; Maurya Simon, who has guided me as a mother would guide.

I am thankful for the hearts and minds of the following individuals: Marina Sanusi, Adam Davis, Rob Ostrom, Susana Romero, Monica Wendel, Emily Hockaday, Jackie Sherbow, Adam Dressler, Javier Zamora, Dara Barnat, Willy Palomo, Amanda Pennelly, Christina Marquez, Marcos A. Quiñones, Ricky Maldonado, Cornelius Eady, Jennifer Ortega, Elsbeth Pancrazi, Monica Sok, Carrie Cooper-Rider, Mitch Jackson, Robb Todd, Kimberly King-Parsons, Sivan Butler-Rotholz, Shannon Humphrey, Steven Cordova, Sarah Wetzel, Jorge Novoa, Nicole Callahan, Manuel Paul López, Monica Sok, Laurie Ann Guerrero, David Campos, Aracelis Girmay, Marco Fernando-Navarro, Roberta Ordona-Cordova, Adam Deutsch, Timothy Donnelly, Miguel Hernandez, sensual(con)sensual.

Much gratitude to the following programs and institutions: Hedgebrook, CantoMundo, Macondo, Bread Loaf, Casa Libre, Napa Valley Writers' Conference, The Anderson Center, The Freya Project, the James D. Phelan Foundation, Letras Latina, Center for Book Arts and the National Endowment for the Arts. Gracias to Peter Conners and the BOA team, who have shown this book (and me) such patience and care.

Thank you to my family, In Lak'ech: you are my other me.

And to the mountains we must all climb to reach the other side.

About the Author

Diana Marie Delgado is the author of the chapbook *Late Night Ta.*
with Men I Think I Trust (Center for Book Arts, 2015). A Nation
Endowment for the Arts fellow and recipient of numerous scholarshi
and grants, she currently resides in Tucson where she is the Litera
Director of the Poetry Center at the University of Arizona. She hol(
MFA degrees in poetry from both Columbia University and th
University of California, Riverside.

BOA Editions, Ltd.
The A. Poulin, Jr. New Poets of America Series

No. 1   *Cedarhome*
         Poems by Barton Sutter
         Foreword by W. D. Snodgrass

No. 2   *Beast Is a Wolf with Brown Fire*
         Poems by Barry Wallenstein
         Foreword by M. L. Rosenthal

No. 3   *Along the Dark Shore*
         Poems by Edward Byrne
         Foreword by John Ashbery

No. 4   *Anchor Dragging*
         Poems by Anthony Piccione
         Foreword by Archibald MacLeish

No. 5   *Eggs in the Lake*
         Poems by Daniela Gioseffi
         Foreword by John Logan

No. 6   *Moving the House*
         Poems by Ingrid Wendt
         Foreword by William Stafford

No. 7   *Whomp and Moonshiver*
         Poems by Thomas Whitbread
         Foreword by Richard Wilbur

No. 8   *Where We Live*
         Poems by Peter Makuck
         Foreword by Louis Simpson

No. 9   *Rose*
         Poems by Li-Young Lee
         Foreword by Gerald Stern

No. 10   *Genesis*
         Poems by Emanuel di Pasquale
         Foreword by X. J. Kennedy

No. 11   *Borders*
         Poems by Mary Crow
         Foreword by David Ignatow

No. 12   *Awake*
         Poems by Dorianne Laux
         Foreword by Philip Levine

No. 13   *Hurricane Walk*
         Poems by Diann Blakely Shoaf
         Foreword by William Matthews

Colophon

BOA Editions, Ltd., a not-for-profit publisher of poetry and other literary works, fosters readership and appreciation of contemporary literature. By identifying, cultivating, and publishing both new and established poets and selecting authors of unique literary talent, BOA brings high-quality literature to the public. Support for this effort comes from the sale of its publications, grant funding, and private donations.

*The publication of this book is made possible, in part,
by the support of the following patrons:*

Anonymous
Angela Bonazinga & Catherine Lewis
Gary & Gwen Conners
Robert L. Giron
James Long Hale
Sandi Henschel, *in honor of Boo Poulin*
John & Barbara Lovenheim
Joe McElveney
Boo Poulin
Deborah Ronnen
Steven O. Russell & Phyllis Rifkin-Russell
William Waddell & Linda Rubel